# Remembering My Child

By

_____

Healing Hearts
Memorial Memoir

Remembering My Child
Healing Hearts Memorial Memoir

Cover Design by AlyBlue Media, LLC
Illustrations by Denise Purcell
Interior Design by AlyBlue Media LLC
Published by AlyBlue Media, LLC
Copyright © 2016 by AlyBlue Media All rights reserved. No part of this publication may be reproduced, distributed or transmitted in any form or by any means, without prior written permission of the publisher.

ISBN: 978-1-944328-45-0

AlyBlue Media, LLC
Ferndale, WA 98248
www.AlyBlueMedia.com

This memorial memoir is designed to provide informative details about our loved ones. It is sold with the understanding that the writer nor publisher is not engaged to render any type of psychological, legal, or any other kind of professional advice. The content is the sole expression and opinion of the writer. No warranties or guarantees are expressed or implied by the choice to include any of the content in this memorial memoir. The publisher shall not be liable for any physical, psychological, emotional, financial, or commercial damages including but not limited to special, incidental, consequential or other damages. You are responsible for your own choices, actions and results.

PRINTED IN THE UNITED STATES OF AMERICA

# Remembering My Child

In loving memory

of

_____

_____
Birth date

_____
Death date

Affix photo of your child here.

REMEMBERING MY CHILD

# Remembering My Child

**PART 1: THE BEFORE**

| | | |
|---|---|---|
| 1 | My Beginning | 1 |
| 2 | About Me | 9 |
| 3 | My Child's Beginning | 15 |
| 4 | My Child's Primary Years | 23 |
| 5 | My Child's Middle Years | 31 |
| 6 | My Child's Teen Years | 39 |
| 7 | The Little Details | 49 |

**PART 2: THE AFTER**

| | | |
|---|---|---|
| 8 | My Loss | 59 |
| 9 | My Child's Memorial | 63 |
| 10 | The Aftermath | 69 |
| 11 | The Belongings | 75 |
| 12 | The Transition | 81 |
| 13 | Birthdays & Angelversaries | 87 |
| 14 | The Holidays | 93 |
| 15 | Our Family | 97 |
| 16 | The Friends | 101 |
| 17 | The Darkness | 105 |
| 18 | My Faith | 111 |
| 19 | My Health | 115 |
| 20 | The Quiet | 119 |
| 21 | My Fears | 123 |
| 22 | My Comfort | 127 |
| 23 | My Silver Lining | 131 |
| 24 | My Hope | 135 |
| 25 | My Journey | 139 |

## INSTRUCTIONS

Writing a memorial memoir harnesses the power of expressive writing to help you capture and preserve details about your child's life. It satisfies an inherent need to ensure that our child's life mattered, and the finished memoir will become a historic record for future generations of your family.

Because every memoir begins with the backstory, this workbook is divided into two parts. It begins with a detailed account of your life, moves into your child's life, and finishes with your own poignant account of losing your child and the aftermath. As you write, allow the questions to prompt you to explore the deepest feelings about your child and your experience through the before and after.

HINT: Penning a memoir shouldn't be done overnight. While cathartic for many, writing about loss can be very hard, especially when tender emotions or memories rise to the surface. It's important to take your time and not rush through. If needed, step back for a while and return to writing when you feel stronger. Keep your own well-being at the forefront at all times.

Penning your memoir:

1. Designate a serene space as your writing spot, a place where you can sit quietly, reflect on your thoughts, and pen your answers undisturbed such as a comfy chair in the corner of your living room, underneath a majestic oak tree at the park, or a quiet spot in your own garden. Write your answers using a favorite pen.

2. Avoid generalized or one-word answers. Record as many details as possible while you still remember them. If a question doesn't apply, skip over it. If you draw a blank or get writer's block, come back to that question later.

3. If your answers change or fresh details come to light, simply add in the space provided.

Using the computer:

1. Using this workbook's questions as your guide, type your answers on your computer. Save your answers as you go. Add and revise as needed when more details surface.

2. Avoid generalized or one-word answers. Record as many details as possible while you still remember them. If a question doesn't apply, skip over it. If you draw a blank or get writer's block, come back to that question later.

3. Once you've completed your memoir on the computer, print and inexpensively bind at an office supply store. You can also self-publish your memoir for free via Amazon (www.CreateSpace.com) or other online venue. To publish professionally, visit AlyBlue Media (www.AlyBlueMedia.com).

# Part 1:

# The Before

REMEMBERING MY CHILD

# My Beginning

A baby is born with a need to be loved,
and never outgrows it.  -FRANK A. CLARK

Every memoir begins with a backstory. In this chapter, describe your own life using the prompts below. If a question doesn't apply, skip over it or come back later but remember that these are details future generations of your family will want to know.

I was born: _____
_____
_____
_____
_____

I was raised: _____
_____
_____
_____
_____
_____
_____

I lived with: _____
_____
_____
_____
_____
_____
_____

# REMEMBERING MY CHILD

About my parents: _____

About my sibling(s): _____

About my maternal grandparents: _____

About my paternal grandparents: _____

About other relatives: _____

# REMEMBERING MY CHILD

My childhood nicknames: _____
_____
_____
_____
_____
_____

About my childhood pets: _____
_____
_____
_____
_____
_____
_____

About my elementary school: _____
_____
_____
_____
_____
_____
_____

About my childhood best friend(s): _____
_____
_____
_____
_____
_____
_____

About my middle school: _____
_____
_____
_____
_____
_____
_____

# REMEMBERING MY CHILD

About my middle school best friend(s): _____
_____
_____
_____
_____
_____
_____
_____

About my high school: _____
_____
_____
_____
_____
_____
_____
_____

About my high school best friend(s): _____
_____
_____
_____
_____
_____
_____
_____

About my first car: _____
_____
_____
_____
_____

About my first job: _____
_____
_____
_____
_____

# REMEMBERING MY CHILD

What I loved most about my childhood: _____

What I least liked about my childhood: _____

What I want others to know about my childhood is: _____

Some of my most memorable childhood experiences were: _____

REMEMBERING MY CHILD

Affix childhood photos of yourself here.

*Notes, thoughts & doodles:*

When we're brave, we make others brave.
Brave is beautiful.
—LYNDA CHELDELIN FELL

# About Me

There is a bright future for you at every turn,
even if you miss one. -UNKNOWN

My birth name is: _____

My current name is: _____

My birthdate is: _____

My birthplace is: _____

My natural hair color is: _____

My current hair color is: _____

My eye color is: _____

My shoe size is: _____

My current clothing size is: _____

My marital status is: _____

My children include: _____
_____
_____
_____
_____

# REMEMBERING MY CHILD

My pet's include: _____
_____
_____
_____
_____

I am fluent in these languages: _____
_____
_____

My current occupation is:: _____
_____
_____

My past occupation(s) is: _____
_____
_____

I attended this college/trade school: _____
_____
_____

I have this certification/degree: _____
_____
_____
_____
_____

I have received these awards: _____
_____
_____
_____

I belong to these organizations: _____
_____
_____

My hobbies include: _____
_____
_____
_____
_____

My volunteer work includes: _____
_____
_____
_____
_____

My body art includes: _____
_____
_____
_____
_____
_____

Other things about me: _____
_____
_____
_____
_____
_____
_____
_____
_____
_____
_____
_____
_____
_____
_____

REMEMBERING MY CHILD

Today's date is: _____

REMEMBERING MY CHILD

Affix current photos of yourself here.

*Notes, thoughts & doodles:*

Compassion and hope are always in season.
-LYNDA CHELDELIN FELL

REMEMBERING MY CHILD

# My Child's Beginning

Having a baby is a life-changer. It gives you a whole other perspective on why you wake up every day. -TAYLOR HANSON

Beginning with the pregnancy, tell us about your child. Was your child planned? Was s/he conceived naturally or via fertility treatment? No detail is too small. If a question doesn't apply, skip over it or come back later.

My child was conceived: _____
_____
_____

At the time of my pregnancy, I lived and worked: _____
_____
_____
_____
_____
_____
_____
_____
_____

The happiest part(s) of the pregnancy were: _____
_____
_____
_____
_____
_____
_____
_____
_____

The hardest part(s) of the pregnancy were: _____

_____
_____
_____
_____
_____
_____
_____
_____
_____

The most memorable part(s) of my pregnancy were: _____

_____
_____
_____
_____
_____
_____
_____
_____

The most memorable part(s) of my child's labor and delivery were: _____

_____
_____
_____
_____
_____
_____
_____
_____
_____
_____
_____
_____
_____
_____
_____
_____

# REMEMBERING MY CHILD

When my child was born, I remember feeling these emotions: _____

_____
_____
_____
_____
_____
_____
_____
_____
_____
_____
_____

As a baby and toddler, the best part(s) of my child's personality were: _____

_____
_____
_____
_____
_____
_____
_____
_____
_____

As a baby and toddler, the challenging part(s) of my child's personality were: _____

_____
_____
_____
_____
_____
_____
_____
_____
_____
_____
_____
_____

# REMEMBERING MY CHILD

As a baby and toddler, my child's favorite pet(s) was: _____
_____
_____
_____

As a baby and toddler, my child's favorite toy(s) was: _____
_____
_____
_____
_____
_____
_____
_____

As a baby and toddler, my child's favorite food(s) was: _____
_____
_____
_____
_____
_____
_____

As a baby and toddler, my child's least favorite food(s) was: _____
_____
_____
_____
_____
_____
_____

As a baby and toddler, my child had these playmates: _____
_____
_____
_____
_____
_____

# REMEMBERING MY CHILD

As a baby and toddler, my child's favorite relative(s) was: _____

_____
_____
_____
_____
_____
_____

As a baby and toddler, my child's favorite activity(s) was: _____

_____
_____
_____
_____
_____
_____

As a baby and toddler, my child's favorite television show(s) was: _____

_____
_____
_____
_____

As a baby and toddler, my child's favorite song(s) was: _____

_____
_____

As a baby and toddler, what I loved most about my child was: _____

_____
_____
_____
_____
_____
_____
_____
_____

# REMEMBERING MY CHILD

What I want others to know about my child: _____

# REMEMBERING MY CHILD

Affix baby/toddler photos of your child here.

*Notes, thoughts & doodles:*

The power to heal is all in the hug.
-LYNDA CHELDELIN FELL

REMEMBERING MY CHILD

# My Child's Primary Years

What makes a child gifted and talented may not
always be good grades in school, but a different way
of looking at the world and learning.  -CHUCK GRASSLEY

Many of our child's precious milestones occur during the formative school years. No matter whether s/he was a quick learner or persevered with learning disabilities, the years spent in primary education offer a treasure trove of memories worthy of recording. No detail is too small. If a question doesn't apply, skip over it or come back later.

My child attended this elementary/primary school(s): _____
_____
_____
_____
_____

My child's favorite elementary teacher was: _____
_____
_____
_____
_____
_____
_____
_____
_____

My child's least favorite elementary teacher was: _____
_____
_____
_____
_____
_____

REMEMBERING MY CHILD

My child's favorite elementary subject(s) was: _____

_____
_____
_____
_____
_____
_____

My child's least favorite elementary subject(s) was: _____

_____
_____
_____
_____
_____
_____

My child's learning style was: _____

_____
_____
_____
_____
_____
_____

The most memorable part(s) of my child's elementary years were: _____

_____
_____
_____
_____
_____
_____
_____
_____
_____
_____
_____
_____
_____
_____

The hardest part(s) of my child's elementary years were: _____

During these school years, the best part(s) of my child's personality were: _____

During these school years, the challenging part(s) of my child's personality were: _____

During these years, my child's favorite color(s) was: _____

REMEMBERING MY CHILD

During these years, my child's favorite pet(s) was: _____
_____
_____
_____
_____
_____
_____
_____
_____
_____

During these years, my child's favorite toy(s) was: _____
_____
_____
_____
_____
_____
_____
_____
_____

During these years, my child's favorite food(s) was: _____
_____
_____
_____
_____
_____
_____

My child's favorite elementary school friend(s) was: _____
_____
_____
_____
_____
_____
_____
_____

## REMEMBERING MY CHILD

During these years, my child's favorite activity(s) was: _____
_____
_____
_____
_____
_____
_____
_____
_____
_____

During these years, my child's favorite sport(s) was: _____
_____
_____
_____
_____

During these years, my child's favorite television show(s) was: _____
_____
_____
_____

During these years, my child's favorite movie(s) was: _____
_____
_____
_____

During these years, my child's favorite song(s) was: _____
_____
_____
_____

During these years, my child received these awards: _____
_____
_____
_____

**During these years, what I loved most about my child was:** _____
_____
_____
_____
_____
_____
_____
_____
_____
_____
_____
_____
_____
_____
_____
_____
_____
_____
_____

**During these years, what I found most challenging about my child was:** _____
_____
_____
_____
_____
_____
_____
_____
_____
_____
_____
_____
_____
_____
_____
_____
_____
_____
_____

# REMEMBERING MY CHILD

Affix photos of your child here.

*Notes, thoughts & doodles:*

Obstacles are merely possibilities in disguise.
-LYNDA CHELDELIN FELL

# My Child's Middle Years

*There were times when, in middle school and junior high,
I didn't have a lot of friends. But my mom was
always my friend. Always.* -TAYLOR SWIFT

The middle school years are a bridge between childhood and adulthood, and is a critical period when children learn their own personal value system, uncover different passions, and discover who they are. What was your child's middle years like? No detail is too small. If a question doesn't apply, skip over it or come back later.

My child attended this middle/junior high school(s): _____
_____
_____
_____
_____

During these years, my child's favorite teacher was: _____
_____
_____
_____
_____
_____
_____
_____
_____

During these years, my child's least favorite teacher was: _____
_____
_____
_____
_____
_____

During these years, my child's favorite subject(s) was: _____

_____
_____
_____
_____
_____

During these years, my child's least favorite subject(s) was: _____

_____
_____
_____
_____
_____

During these years, my child's learning style was: _____

_____
_____
_____
_____
_____

The most memorable part(s) of my child's middle years were: _____

_____
_____
_____
_____
_____
_____
_____
_____
_____
_____
_____
_____

# REMEMBERING MY CHILD

The hardest part(s) of my child's middle years were: _____

_____
_____
_____
_____
_____
_____
_____
_____
_____
_____

During these years, the best part(s) of my child's personality were: _____

_____
_____
_____
_____
_____
_____
_____
_____
_____
_____

During these years, the challenging part(s) of my child's personality were: _____

_____
_____
_____
_____
_____
_____
_____

During these years, my child's favorite color(s) was: _____

_____
_____
_____
_____
_____
_____

During these years, my child's favorite pet(s) was: _____

During these years, my child's favorite Item(s) was: _____

During these years, my child's favorite food(s) was: _____

During these years, my child's favorite friend(s) was: _____

# REMEMBERING MY CHILD

During these years, my child's favorite activity(s) was: _____

_____
_____
_____
_____
_____
_____
_____
_____
_____
_____

During these years, my child's favorite sport(s) was: _____

_____
_____
_____
_____

During these years, my child's favorite television show(s) was: _____

_____
_____
_____

During these years, my child's favorite movie(s) was: _____

_____
_____
_____

During these years, my child's favorite music genre(s) was: _____

_____
_____
_____

During these years, my child received these awards: _____

_____
_____
_____
_____

**During these years, what I loved most about my child was:** _____
_____
_____
_____
_____
_____
_____
_____
_____
_____
_____
_____
_____
_____
_____
_____
_____
_____
_____
_____

**During these years, what I found most challenging about my child was:** _____
_____
_____
_____
_____
_____
_____
_____
_____
_____
_____
_____
_____
_____
_____
_____
_____
_____
_____
_____

# REMEMBERING MY CHILD

Affix photos of your child here.

*Notes, thoughts & doodles:*

Bloom where you are planted.
-LYNDA CHELDELIN FELL

REMEMBERING MY CHILD

# My Child's Teen Years

Fitting in is unnecessary. Embrace who you are.
-NEON HITCH

Filled with growth spurts and puberty changes, our child's teen years are a time of intense transition. The physical and psychological development that takes place before finally arriving at the doorstep of legal adulthood can offer both the best of times as well as the most challenging. What was your child's teen years like? No detail is too small. If a question doesn't apply, skip over it or come back later.

My child attended this high school(s): _____
_____
_____
_____
_____
_____

As a teen, my child's favorite teacher was: _____
_____
_____
_____
_____
_____
_____
_____

As a teen, my child's least favorite teacher was: _____
_____
_____
_____
_____

As a teen, my child's favorite subject(s) was: _____

As a teen, my child's least favorite subject(s) was: _____

As a teen, my child's learning style was: _____

The most memorable part(s) of my child's teen years were: _____

The hardest part(s) of my child's teen years were: _____

As a teen, the best part(s) of my child's personality were: _____

As a teen, the challenging part(s) of my child's personality were: _____

As a teen, my child struggled the most with: _____

REMEMBERING MY CHILD

As a teen, my child's favorite color(s) was: _____
_____
_____
_____

As a teen, my child's favorite pet(s) was: _____
_____
_____
_____
_____
_____
_____
_____

As a teen, my child's favorite Item(s) was: _____
_____
_____
_____
_____
_____
_____
_____

As a teen, my child's favorite food(s) was: _____
_____
_____
_____
_____
_____
_____
_____

My child's favorite snack was: _____
_____
_____
_____
_____

# REMEMBERING MY CHILD

As a teen, my child's favorite friend(s) was: _____

As a teen, my child's favorite sport(s) was: _____

As a teen, my child's favorite activity(s) was: _____

As a teen, my child's favorite hobby(s) was: _____

As a teen, my child's favorite book(s) was: _____

REMEMBERING MY CHILD

As a teen, my child's favorite television show(s) was: _____
_____
_____
_____

As a teen, my child's favorite movie(s) was: _____
_____
_____
_____

As a teen, my child's favorite music genre(s) was: _____
_____
_____
_____

As a teen, my child received these awards: _____
_____
_____
_____

As a teen, my child volunteered with: _____
_____
_____
_____

My child's first employment was: _____
_____
_____
_____
_____
_____

REMEMBERING MY CHILD

My child's first car or favorite transportation was: _____

During these years, what I found most challenging about my child was: _____

**During these years, what I loved most about my child was:**

# REMEMBERING MY CHILD

Affix photos of your child here.

*Notes, thoughts & doodles:*

Not every day is beautiful, but there is beauty in every day.
-LYNDA CHELDELIN FELL

REMEMBERING MY CHILD

# The Little Details

*Moments are fleeting, memories are permanent, love is forever.*
-LYNDA CHELDELIN FELL

On the following pages are tidbits about your child that offer a snapshot of who s/he was, and what you want future generations of your family to know.

My child's eye color was: _____
_____

My child's natural hair color was: _____
_____

My child's height was: _____
_____

My child's weight was: _____
_____

My child's clothing size was: _____
_____

My child's shoe size was: _____
_____

My child's clothing style was: _____
_____
_____
_____

My child's body art included: _____
_____

# REMEMBERING MY CHILD

My child had a: _____

_____

_____

_____

Example: Good heart, gentle soul, witty personality

My child made a good: _____

_____

_____

_____

Example: Good lasagna, potato salad, scrapbook, quilt

My child was a good: _____

_____

_____

_____

Example: Friend, gardener, knitter, painter, poem writer, helper, leader

People would say my child was: _____

_____

_____

_____

Example: Funny, kind, smart, gentle, generous, humble, creative

My child's talents included: _____

_____

_____

_____

Example: Finding things, good memory, witty comments, applying makeup, keeping room tidy, etc.

My child loved to: _____

_____

_____

_____

Example: Take baths, drink cocoa before bed, wear cushy socks, light a fragrant candle, go to the beach, etc.

REMEMBERING MY CHILD

My child's favorite book or book genre was:_____

_____
_____
_____
_____

Example: Harry Potter series, romance, science fiction, home decorating

My child's favorite scent or fragrance was:_____

_____
_____
_____
_____
_____

Example: Citrus, sugar cookies, seashore, Victoria Secret perfume, Hugo Boss cologne, fresh-cut grass

My child's favorite song or band was:_____

_____
_____
_____
_____
_____

My child's favorite hobby was:_____

_____
_____
_____
_____

Example: Beading, woodworking, magic tricks, bike riding, scrapbooking, rock collecting, fishing, etc.

My child's favorite game was:_____

_____
_____
_____
_____

Example: Monopoly, Hide 'n Seek, Go Fish, Scrabble, Pokemon, video games, etc.

# REMEMBERING MY CHILD

My child's favorite store was:_____
_____
_____
_____
_____
_____

Example: Dollar Store, the mall, Victoria Secret, Cabelas, Wal-Mart, Target, Nordstroms, etc.

My child's favorite vacation was:_____
_____
_____
_____
_____
_____

My child was most like me in these ways:_____
_____
_____
_____
_____
_____
_____
_____
_____
_____
_____
_____

My child was different from me in these ways:_____
_____
_____
_____
_____
_____
_____
_____

My child made a difference in the world because:

Things I don't want to forget about my child include:

# REMEMBERING MY CHILD

Affix photos of your child here.

REMEMBERING MY CHILD

Affix photos of your child here.

*Notes, thoughts & doodles:*

The heart can hold joy at the same time it holds sorrow.
-LYNDA CHELDELIN FELL

# Part 2:

## The After

## My Loss

Grievers use a very simple calendar. Before and after.
-LYNDA CHELDELIN FELL

In order to fully understand our journey through loss, it is helpful to start at the pivotal moment that defines our before and after.

My child died on:_____
_____

Where I was and what I was doing when it happened: _____
_____
_____
_____
_____
_____
_____

What happened: _____
_____
_____
_____
_____
_____
_____
_____
_____
_____

*Notes, thoughts & doodles:*

We survive grief one breath at a time.
-LYNDA CHELDELIN FELL

# My Child's Memorial

It's okay to cry. When you're in the middle of the moment, when you can't stop crying, there is fear that the pain will never end. But allowing yourself those moments are an important part of the healing. -LYNDA CHELDELIN FELL

Planning our child's memorial presents emotionally-laden challenges shared by every parent. Choosing between cremation or a casket, picking a burial plot, holding a private unofficial remembrance or going with a full traditional funeral are but a few of the decisions we face. How do we get through the day, hour, minute? Use this chapter to record every detail.

The date of my child's memorial was: _____

This date was chosen because: _____

I chose a cremation or burial because: _____

The people who helped plan the memorial included: _____

_____
_____
_____
_____
_____
_____
_____
_____
_____

The service was held at: _____

_____
_____
_____
_____
_____

The service was presided over by: _____

_____
_____
_____
_____
_____

The people who spoke at my child's service included: _____

_____
_____
_____
_____
_____
_____
_____
_____
_____

# REMEMBERING MY CHILD

The music we selected was: _____
_____
_____
_____
_____
_____
_____
_____
_____
_____
_____

The poems, scriptures, readings we selected were: _____
_____
_____
_____
_____
_____
_____
_____

During my child's service, I didn't expect: _____
_____
_____
_____
_____
_____
_____
_____
_____
_____
_____

The most memorable parts of my child's service were: _____
_____
_____
_____
_____
_____
_____

REMEMBERING MY CHILD

# REMEMBERING MY CHILD

*Notes, thoughts & doodles:*

Hugs are nourishment for the heart.
LYNDA CHELDELIN FELL

# The Aftermath

*Just as it's impossible to explain childbirth to a person
who has never given birth, it is impossible to explain
child loss to a person who has never lost a child.*
-LYNDA CHELDELIN FELL

In the aftermath of loss, the intensity of our emotions and overwhelming sorrow threaten to engulf us and we wonder how we're going to survive such devastation. What do you remember from the first days, weeks and months after the loss of your child? What emotions do you recall? How did you cope?

In the first days, weeks and months after my child's death, I felt: _____
_____
_____
_____
_____
_____
_____
_____
_____
_____
_____
_____
_____
_____
_____
_____
_____
_____
_____
_____
_____
_____

# REMEMBERING MY CHILD

**In the first days, weeks and months after my child's death, I remember:** _____

In the first days, weeks and months after my child's death, I coped by: _____

My family coped by: _____

What I remember most from this time: _____

*Notes, thoughts & doodles:*

Loss has a way of waking us up to what's truly important.
LYNDA CHELDELIN FELL

REMEMBERING MY CHILD

# The Belongings

Of all possessions, a friend is the most precious.
-HERODOTUS

At some point we're faced with the task of sorting through our child's belongings. Whether we tend to this task immediately or put it off for years, every item large and small holds memories and we're faced with deciding what to keep, what to stow away, and what to donate or discard. When does the time come to address such an emotionally-laden task and how do we begin?

I sorted through my child's belongings on: _____
_____
_____
_____
_____
_____
_____
_____
_____
_____
_____
_____
_____
_____
_____

My child's favorite article of clothing was: _____
_____
_____
_____
_____
_____

# REMEMBERING MY CHILD

My child's favorite outfit included: _____

_____

_____

_____

_____

_____

_____

_____

_____

_____

_____

_____

_____

_____

My child's favorite items included: _____

_____

_____

_____

_____

_____

_____

_____

_____

_____

_____

_____

_____

_____

_____

_____

_____

My most cherished items include: _____

_____
_____
_____
_____
_____
_____
_____
_____
_____
_____
_____
_____

The items I kept as keepsakes included: _____

_____
_____
_____
_____
_____
_____
_____
_____
_____
_____
_____
_____
_____
_____
_____
_____
_____
_____
_____
_____
_____
_____
_____
_____

REMEMBERING MY CHILD

The items I donated included: _____
_____
_____
_____
_____
_____
_____
_____
_____
_____
_____
_____
_____
_____
_____
_____
_____
_____
_____
_____

The items I discarded included: _____
_____
_____
_____
_____
_____
_____
_____
_____
_____
_____
_____
_____
_____
_____
_____
_____
_____
_____

The hardest part about this task was: _____

These people helped me: _____

*Notes, thoughts & doodles:*

Age may wrinkle the face, but lack of compassion wrinkles the heart.
LYNDA CHELDELIN FELL

## The Transition

The bereaved need more than just the space to grieve the loss.
They also need the space to grieve the transition.
-LYNDA CHELDELIN FELL

At some point following the loss of our child, we are faced with returning to a routine. Whether it be work, school, or caring for our family, transitioning from our old life to one without our child marks the period between what once was a familiar routine to new, unfamiliar territory.

After my child died, getting out of bed was: _____
_____
_____
_____
_____
_____
_____
_____
_____
_____
_____
_____
_____
_____

I took this many days off before returning to school/work: _____
_____
_____
_____
_____
_____

When I returned to school/work, the emotions I felt included: _____

My colleagues/ classmates/teachers treated me: _____

What I wished they had known or done differently was: _____

My family handled this transition by: _____

_____
_____
_____
_____
_____
_____
_____
_____
_____
_____

The hardest part about this transition period was: _____

_____
_____
_____
_____
_____
_____
_____
_____
_____

The people who supported me/my family the most during this transition included: _____

_____
_____
_____
_____
_____
_____
_____
_____
_____
_____
_____
_____
_____
_____
_____

REMEMBERING MY CHILD

What I remember most about this time was: _____

# REMEMBERING MY CHILD

*Notes, thoughts & doodles:*

Healed people heal people.
LYNDA CHELDELIN FELL

REMEMBERING MY CHILD

# Birthday & Angelversary

*Giving in to the tears is like freefalling without a parachute. But it's vital to our well-being as we process the deep anguish.*
- LYNDA CHELDELIN FELL

Our child's birthday and death anniversary are predictably painful. No matter how long it's been, fresh waves of sorrow fill our hearts as if it happened yesterday. Some parents choose to spend the day in solitude, lost in memory about the moment his or her child came into this world, and the moment he or she left. Others choose to mark the dates with a remembrance activity such as a balloon release. How do we celebrate the life that lives on in our heart? How do we mark the date of our child's departure?

My child was born on: _____

My child's favorite way to celebrate his or her birthday was: _____
_____
_____
_____
_____
_____
_____
_____
_____
_____
_____
_____
_____
_____
_____
_____
_____
_____

My child's most memorable birthday(s) was:

# REMEMBERING MY CHILD

The first year after my child died, I chose to honor his/her birthday this way: _____

_____
_____
_____
_____
_____
_____
_____
_____
_____
_____
_____
_____
_____
_____

Now I mark my child's birthday this way: _____

_____
_____
_____
_____
_____
_____
_____
_____
_____
_____
_____
_____
_____
_____

The people who join me in my remembrance are: _____

_____
_____
_____
_____
_____
_____
_____
_____

# REMEMBERING MY CHILD

My child died on: _____
_____
_____
_____
_____
_____
_____
_____

The first year after my child died, I chose to honor the angelversary this way: _____
_____
_____
_____
_____
_____
_____
_____
_____
_____
_____
_____
_____

Now I mark my child's angelversary this way: _____
_____
_____
_____
_____
_____
_____
_____
_____
_____
_____
_____
_____
_____
_____

# REMEMBERING MY CHILD

The people who join me in my remembrance are: _____

_____
_____
_____
_____
_____
_____
_____

The hardest part about my child's birthday is: _____

_____
_____
_____
_____
_____
_____
_____
_____
_____
_____
_____
_____

The hardest part about my child's angelversary is: _____

_____
_____
_____
_____
_____
_____
_____
_____
_____
_____
_____
_____
_____
_____

*Notes, thoughts & doodles:*

I aspire to be a giver; a giver of good hugs,
a giver of love, and a giver of hope.
LYNDA CHELDELIN FELL

REMEMBERING MY CHILD

## The Holidays

The only predictable thing about grief is that it's unpredictable.
- LYNDA CHELDELIN FELL

The holidays come around like clockwork, yet treasured memories from years past can expectedly trigger a fresh wave of sorrow. If the grief is still fresh, holidays can be downright raw. How do we navigate the invitations, decorations, and festivities without our precious child?

My child's favorite holiday(s) was: _____

_____

_____

_____


My child's favorite way to celebrate this holiday was: _____

_____

_____

_____

_____

_____

_____

_____


My most memorable holiday with my child was: _____

_____

_____

_____

_____

_____

_____

_____

REMEMBERING MY CHILD

The first year after my child died, I chose to honor his/her favorite holiday this way: _____
_____
_____
_____
_____
_____
_____
_____
_____
_____
_____
_____
_____
_____

Now I mark my child's favorite holiday this way: _____
_____
_____
_____
_____
_____
_____
_____
_____
_____
_____
_____
_____
_____

The people who join me in my remembrance are: _____
_____
_____
_____
_____
_____
_____
_____
_____

# REMEMBERING MY CHILD

The hardest holiday for me now is: _____

_____
_____
_____
_____
_____
_____
_____
_____
_____
_____
_____
_____
_____
_____

I find that holiday hardest because: _____

_____
_____
_____
_____
_____
_____
_____
_____
_____
_____
_____
_____
_____
_____

The people who help me the most through this holiday are: _____

_____
_____
_____
_____
_____
_____
_____

*Notes, thoughts & doodles:*

Some days are just hard, but there is always hope in tomorrow.
LYNDA CHELDELIN FELL

REMEMBERING MY CHILD

# Our Family

> Happy or unhappy, families are all mysterious. We have only to imagine how differently we would be described - and will be, after our deaths - by each of the family members who believe they know us. -GLORIA STEINEM

In the aftermath of losing a child, our entire family is impacted. Although bound by relations, we are all wired differently, and process loss in our own unique way. How was your family impacted by the loss of your child?

The family relationship(s) that has been impacted the most is:_____

_____
_____
_____
_____
_____
_____
_____
_____
_____
_____
_____
_____
_____
_____
_____
_____
_____
_____
_____
_____

REMEMBERING MY CHILD

The family member(s) who stood by me the most are: _____

_____

The family member(s) who stood by me the least are: _____

# REMEMBERING MY CHILD

What I want my family to know about the loss of my child is:

*Notes, thoughts & doodles:*

Everyone wants to be the sun to light someone's world.
But why not be the moon to light someone's darkness?
LYNDA CHELDELIN FELL

# Our Friends

Remember, you don't need a certain number of friends,
just a number of friends you can be certain of.   -UNKNOWN

In the aftermath of losing a child, friendships naturally shift. Some are strengthened as those friends offer a shoulder as a safe haven for our tears, while others fail us and fall away. How did your friends react to the loss of your child?

The friendship(s) that has been impacted the most is:_____
_____
_____
_____
_____
_____
_____
_____
_____
_____
_____
_____
_____
_____
_____
_____
_____
_____
_____
_____
_____
_____
_____

The friend(s) who stood by me the most are: _____

_____


The friend(s) who stood by me the least are: _____

_____

# REMEMBERING MY CHILD

What I want my friends to know about the loss of my child is:

*Notes, thoughts & doodles:*

Every dawn holds the power of fresh hope.
LYNDA CHELDELIN FELL

REMEMBERING MY CHILD

## The Darkness

Walking with a friend in the dark is better than
walking alone in the light.  -HELEN KELLER

In the aftermath of losing a child, experiencing dark thoughts is common. While there would be no rainbow without the rain, how do we survive the storm?

After my child died, I experienced these dark thoughts:_____
_____
_____
_____
_____
_____
_____
_____
_____
_____
_____
_____
_____
_____
_____
_____
_____
_____
_____
_____
_____
_____
_____
_____

**These are the emotions I struggled with when I experienced dark thoughts:**

I told my dark thoughts to:_____

_____
_____
_____
_____
_____
_____
_____
_____
_____
_____
_____
_____
_____
_____
_____
_____

Their reaction to my dark thoughts was:_____

_____
_____
_____
_____
_____

I sought help for my dark thoughts this way:_____

_____
_____
_____
_____
_____
_____
_____
_____
_____
_____
_____
_____
_____

My dark thoughts lasted this long:_____

_____
_____
_____
_____
_____
_____
_____
_____
_____
_____

I worked through these dark thoughts by doing these things:_____

_____
_____
_____
_____
_____
_____
_____
_____
_____
_____
_____
_____
_____
_____
_____
_____
_____
_____
_____
_____
_____

**What I want others to know about my dark thoughts is this:**

*Notes, thoughts & doodles:*

She who heals herself heals others.
LYNDA CHELDELIN FELL

REMEMBERING MY CHILD

# My Faith

We have always held to the hope, the belief,
the conviction that there is a better life, a better world,
beyond the horizon. -FRANKLIN D. ROOSEVELT

Grief has far-reaching effects in most areas of our life, including faith. For some, our faith can deepen. For others, it can be a source of disappointment. One commonality among the bereaved is that faith is often altered one way or the other. How has your faith been impacted?

I was raised with this faith:_____
_____
_____
_____
_____
_____
_____
_____
_____
_____
_____
_____
_____
_____

Since my child's death, my faith has been a source of comfort because:_____
_____
_____
_____
_____
_____
_____
_____
_____

My faith has disappointed me in these areas: _____

_____
_____
_____
_____
_____
_____
_____
_____
_____
_____
_____

My faith has since changed in this way: _____

_____
_____
_____
_____
_____
_____
_____
_____
_____
_____

My beliefs have since changed in this way: _____

_____
_____
_____
_____
_____
_____
_____
_____
_____

I wish my faith would change these views about loss and grief:

This is what I want my faith to know about loss and grief:

*Notes, thoughts & doodles:*

I already know sorrow. Today I choose joy.
LYNDA CHELDELIN FELL

REMEMBERING MY CHILD

# My Health

Health is a state of complete physical, mental, and social
well-being, and not merely the absence of disease or infirmity.
-WORLD HEALTH ORGANIZATION

As our anatomical and physiological systems work in tandem with our emotional well-being, when one part of our body is stressed, other parts become compromised. Has your grief affected your physical health?

Prior to my child's death, I considered my health to be: _____
_____
_____
_____
_____
_____
_____
_____
_____
_____
_____
_____


Prior to my child's death, I had these health issues: _____
_____
_____
_____
_____
_____
_____
_____
_____
_____
_____

After my child's death, I developed these health issues: _____
_____
_____
_____
_____
_____
_____
_____
_____
_____
_____
_____

Since my child's death, the area of health that has improved the most is: _____
_____
_____
_____
_____
_____
_____
_____
_____
_____
_____
_____

Since my child's death, these are the steps I've taken to improve my health: _____
_____
_____
_____
_____
_____
_____
_____
_____
_____

Now I consider my health to be: _____

What I want my doctor to know about grief is: _____

What I want others to know about grief and my health is: _____

*Notes, thoughts & doodles:*

One laugh can scatter a hundred griefs.
LYNDA CHELDELIN FELL

# The Quiet

*Heavy hearts, like heavy clouds in the sky, are best relieved by the letting go of a little water.* -ANTOINE RIVAROL

Our child's absence remains day and night, but certain times of the day are harder than others. For some, it is evening or night when the house is quiet. For others, it is morning or afternoon. What time is hardest for you?

In the initial aftermath of my child's death, the hardest time of day for me was:_____

_____
_____
_____
_____
_____
_____
_____
_____
_____
_____
_____
_____
_____
_____
_____
_____
_____
_____
_____
_____
_____

**Now, I find the hardest time of day to be:**

I find this time hard because:

*Notes, thoughts & doodles:*

The beauty of hope is that it has no expiration date.
LYNDA CHELDELIN FELL

REMEMBERING MY CHILD

# My Fears

*You gain strength, courage, and confidence by every experience in which you really stop to look fear in the face. You are able to say to yourself "I lived through this horror. I can take the next thing that comes along."*
-ELEANOR ROOSEVELT

In the aftermath of losing a child, fear can keep us focused on the past or worried about the future. If we can acknowledge our fear, we realize that right now we are okay. How do we control our fear, so it doesn't control us?

Before my child died, I was afraid of:_____
_____
_____
_____
_____
_____
_____


In the initial aftermath of my child's death, my biggest fear became:_____
_____
_____
_____
_____
_____
_____
_____
_____
_____
_____

# REMEMBERING MY CHILD

Now my biggest fear for myself is: _____

_____

_____

_____

_____

_____

_____

_____

_____

_____

_____

My biggest fear for my family is: _____

_____

_____

_____

_____

_____

_____

_____

_____

_____

_____

I manage my fears by doing these things: _____

_____

_____

_____

_____

_____

_____

_____

Some people feel my fears are irrational because:

I feel my fears are rational because::

This is what I want others to know about my fears:

*Notes, thoughts & doodles:*

You're one smile away from a good mood.
LYNDA CHELDELIN FELL

# My Comfort

*Life is made up not of great sacrifices or duties, but of little things, in which smiles and kindness, and small obligations given habitually, are what preserve the heart and secure comfort.* -HUMPHRY DAVY

In the aftermath of loss, what brings comfort one day can bring pain the next. Eventually we find a symbolic item or soothing ritual that offers a balm for the wound in our heart. What items or rituals bring you the most comfort?

When my child died, these items brought me the most comfort: _____
_____
_____
_____
_____
_____
_____
_____
_____
_____

The items that now bring me comfort are: _____
_____
_____
_____
_____
_____
_____
_____
_____
_____

# REMEMBERING MY CHILD

When my child died, these activities brought me the most comfort:

The activities that now bring me comfort are:

When my child died, these rituals brought me the most comfort:

The rituals that now bring me comfort are:

What I want others to know about my need for comfort is:

*Notes, thoughts & doodles:*

Hugs are, and always will be, better than words.
LYNDA CHELDELIN FELL

# My Silver Lining

Even a small star shines in darkness.
-FINNISH PROVERB

In the earliest days following loss, the thought that anything good can come from our experience is beyond comprehension. Yet some say there are blessings in everything, every experience. Have you discovered a silver lining in your loss?

In the aftermath of my child's death, I've discovered these silver linings: _____
_____
_____
_____
_____
_____
_____
_____
_____
_____
_____
_____
_____
_____
_____
_____
_____
_____
_____
_____
_____
_____
_____

**My child's death had a positive impact upon the lives of others in this way:**

I am now most grateful for: _____

*Notes, thoughts & doodles:*

Life is a balance of pain and joy, laughter and tears, hardships and blessings.
LYNDA CHELDELIN FELL

# My Hope

*Be like the birds, sing after every storm.*
-BETH MENDE CONNY

In the aftermath of loss, hope can be hard to find. Yet every sunrise brings with it a ray of hope for a better tomorrow. Is hope possible in the aftermath of losing a child? If so, where do we find it?

Before my child's death, my definition of hope was: _____
_____
_____
_____
_____
_____
_____
_____
_____
_____
_____
_____

Now my definition of hope is: _____
_____
_____
_____
_____
_____
_____
_____
_____
_____
_____
_____

# REMEMBERING MY CHILD

These are the things I hope for myself: _____

_____

_____

_____

_____

_____

_____

_____

_____

_____

_____

_____

_____

_____

_____

_____

These are the things I hope for my family: _____

_____

_____

_____

_____

_____

_____

_____

_____

_____

_____

_____

_____

_____

_____

_____

What I want others to know about hope is:

*Notes, thoughts & doodles:*

The power of one hope can change an entire world.
LYNDA CHELDELIN FELL

# My Journey

*One turn can change your journey, but the final destination is still up to you.* -LYNDA CHELDELIN FELL

Birthing, loving, and then burying a child is a journey that is near impossible to describe. In the final chapter of your memoir, what do you want others to know about you, your child, and your journey through loss? How do you define your future? How do you define love?

Before my child's death, I would describe myself this way: _____
_____
_____
_____
_____
_____
_____
_____
_____
_____
_____
_____
_____

Now I would describe myself this way: _____
_____
_____
_____
_____
_____
_____
_____
_____
_____
_____

My definition of love is:

What I want others to know about my journey is:

*Notes, thoughts & doodles:*

Kind heart, brave voice, compassionate spirit; that's all I aspire to be.
LYNDA CHELDELIN FELL

## ABOUT

# LYNDA CHELDELIN FELL

Considered a pioneer in the field of inspirational hope in the aftermath of loss, Lynda Cheldelin Fell has a passion for creating and producing groundbreaking projects that create a legacy of help, healing, and hope.

She is the award-winning creator of the 5-star book series *Grief Diaries*, board president of the National Grief & Hope Coalition, and CEO of AlyBlue Media. Her repertoire of interviews include Dr. Martin Luther King's daughter, Trayvon Martin's mother, sisters of the late Nicole Brown Simpson, Pastor Todd Burpo of Heaven Is For Real, CNN commentator Dr. Ken Druck, and other societal newsmakers on finding healing and hope in the aftermath of life's harshest challenges.

Lynda's own story began in 2007, when she had an alarming dream about her young teenage daughter, Aly. In the dream, Aly was a backseat passenger in a car that veered off the road and landed in a lake. Aly sank with the car, leaving behind an open book floating face down on the water. Two years later, Lynda's dream became reality when her daughter was killed as a backseat passenger in a car accident while coming home from a swim meet.

Overcome with grief, Lynda's forty-six-year-old husband suffered a major stroke that left him with severe disabilities, changing the family dynamics once again.

The following year, Lynda was invited to share her remarkable story about finding hope after loss and that one cathartic experience inspired her to create ground-breaking projects spanning national events, radio, film and books to help others who share the same journey feel less alone. Lynda created the 5-star Grief Diaries book series featuring true stories about real life experiences, now home to more than 500 writers spanning the globe. Her collection of Healing Hearts Memorial Memoirs invites people of all ages to harness the power of expressive writing to capture and preserve a detailed historical account documenting the life and death a loved one.

lynda@lyndafell.com | www.lyndafell.com | www.griefdiaries.com

## ABOUT

# DENISE PURCELL

Denise Purcell was born in Syracuse, New York, the oldest of seven. She is a published poet, writer and author of *Grief Diaries: Living with D.I.D*, and talented artist with pieces on display around the northeast.

Denise was diagnosed with 17 personalities at age 30, and is currently working towards bringing about a better understanding and awareness of dissociative identity disorder. Since losing her 27-year-old daughter Megan in 2011, Denise has become a strong advocate for many injustices, and uses art to help others view life as a chance to see the beauty in adversity.

REMEMBERING MY CHILD

## ALYBLUE MEDIA TITLES

Available by booksellers around the world
Remembering My Child Memorial Memoir
Remembering My Mother Memorial Memoir
Remembering My Father Memorial Memoir
Remembering My Sister Memorial Memoir
Remembering My Brother Memorial Memoir
Remembering My Husband Memorial Memoir
Remembering My Wife Memorial Memoir
Remembering My Grandmother Memorial Memoir
Remembering My Grandfather Memorial Memoir
Grief Diaries: Surviving Loss of a Spouse
Grief Diaries: Surviving Loss of a Child
Grief Diaries: Surviving Loss of a Sibling
Grief Diaries: Surviving Loss of a Parent
Grief Diaries: Surviving Loss of an Infant
Grief Diaries: Surviving Loss of a Loved One
Grief Diaries: Surviving Loss by Suicide
Grief Diaries: Surviving Loss of Health
Grief Diaries: How to Help the Newly Bereaved
Grief Diaries: Loss by Impaired Driving
Grief Diaries: Through the Eyes of an Eating Disorder
Grief Diaries: Loss by Homicide
Grief Diaries: Loss of a Pregnancy
Grief Diaries: Living with a Brain Injury
Grief Diaries: Hello from Heaven
Grief Diaries: Grieving the Living
Grief Diaries: Shattered
Grief Diaries: Project Cold Case
Grief Diaries: Through the Eyes of Men
Grief Diaries: Living with Mental Illness
Grief Diaries: Living with Endometriosis
Grief Diaries: Through the Eyes of D.I.D.
Grief Diaries: Poetry & Prose and More
Grief Diaries: Life with an Alcoholic
Grief Diaries: Loving an Addict
Grief Diaries: Through the Eyes of a Funeral Director
Grammy Visits From Heaven
Faith, Grief & Pass the Chocolate Pudding
Heaven Talks to Children

**PUBLISHED BY ALYBLUE MEDIA**
Inside every human is a story worth sharing.
www.AlyBlueMedia.com